The Twelve Steps of Phobics Victorious

Rosemary

Copyright © 2016 Rosemary

The Twelve Steps of Phobics Victorious

Phobics Victorious
Founded 1993
1-760-770-0462
rosemaryjane@dc.rr.com

All rights exclusively reserved. No part of this book may be reproduced or translated into any language or utilized in any form or by any means, electronic or mechanical, including photocopying, recording or by any information storage and retrieval system, without permission in writing from the author.

ISBN 978-0-9972085-3-5 (paperback)
ISBN 978-0-9972085-2-8 (ebook)

Published by AquaZebra, www.AquaZebra.com

Author: Rosemary

Book Designer Mark E. Anderson, AquaZebra

www.AquaZebra.com

Library of Congress Control Number: 2016900372

Library of Congress - United States Copyright Office
Certificate of Registration
TXU 602 389

What Is Phobics Victorious?

Phobics Victorious is a Christ centered recovery program and ministry for people suffering and recovering from irrational fears, phobias, and acute panic attacks.

Phobics Victorious is based on the twelve step approach to recovery as used in such fellowships as Alcoholics Anonymous, Narcotics Anonymous, Alcoholics Victorious, and Overcomers.

Phobics Victorious is also a tool by which suffering phobics can learn about our Higher Power, Jesus Christ. In Phobics Victorious, we declare Jesus Christ as our Higher Power. In following the twelve steps of Phobics Victorious, we are led to a knowledge of Jesus Christ as our Lord and Savior.

Through our desire to learn about, and our commitment to Jesus Christ as our Higher Power, and through following Jesus, the Holy Scriptures, and the biblically based twelve steps of Phobics Victorious, we are led into freedom and victory over fear.

Are you a phobic? Ask yourself the following questions to see if you need help in recovering from fear, phobias, and panic attacks and to see if you know Jesus Christ as your personal Savior.

1. Do you ever experience the following symptoms to such an extent that they interfere with your everyday functioning?
   - rapid heartbeat
   - intense fear, panic
   - paralysis of action
   - dread of impending doom
   - embarrassment
   - desire to escape
   - unable to leave your home
   - unable to communicate effectively with others
   - fear of heart attack or going crazy
   - loss of control
   - avoidance of places, people

2. Do you rely on alcohol or drugs to function in phobic situations?

3. Do you worry excessively, catastrophizing, anticipating the worst?

4. Do you lack faith in God or in yourself?

5. Do you know who you are?

6. Do you want to be free from irrational fears and panic attacks?

We in Phobics Victorious look to Jesus Christ for our recovery. We study the word of God, the Holy Bible, and we follow the Christ-centered twelve steps of Phobics Victorious. We fellowship with other suffering, recovering, and freed phobics in Phobics Victorious. We meditate on our daily affirmation book, One Day at a Time in Phobics Victorious.

If you are open minded, honest and willing, the spiritual journey of the twelve steps of Phobics Victorious, with Jesus Christ at the center, will transform your life. One day at a time, as we let go and let God, and surrender our lives to Him, we receive peace, serenity, and freedom. We become new creations in Christ; healthy, whole and free.

> *"I sought the Lord, and He heard me,*
> *and delivered me from all my fears."*
> *Psalms 34:4*

The Twelve Steps of Phobics Victorious

1. We admitted we were powerless over the enemy, fear, and that our lives had become unmanageable.

2. We came to believe that a power greater than ourselves, the Lord Jesus Christ, could restore us to sanity.

3. We made a decision to turn our will and our lives over to the care of God the Father, His Son Jesus Christ and His Holy Spirit.

4. We made a searching and fearless moral inventory of ourselves.

5. We admitted to God, to ourselves, and to another human being, the exact nature of our wrongs.

6. We became entirely ready to have God remove our defects of character.

7. We humbly asked Him to remove our shortcomings.

8. We made a list of all persons we had harmed and became willing to make amends to them all.

9. We made direct amends to such people whenever possible, except when to do so would injure them or others.

10. We continued to take a personal inventory and when we were wrong we promptly admitted it

11. We sought through prayer and meditation to improve our conscious contact with God the Father, His Son Jesus Christ and His Holy Spirit, praying only for knowledge of His will for us and the power to carry that out.

12. Having had a spiritual awakening as the result of these steps, we tried to carry this message to others, and to practice these principles in all our affairs.

THE TWELVE STEPS OF ALCOHOLICS ANONYMOUS:
1. We admitted we were powerless over alcohol - that our lives had become unmanageable. 2. Came to believe that a Power greater than ourselves could restore us to sanity. 3. Made a decision to turn our will and our lives over to the care of God as we understood Him. 4. Made a searching and fearless moral inventory of ourselves. 5. Admitted to God, to ourselves and to another human being the exact nature of our wrongs. 6. Were entirely ready to have God remove all these defects of character. 7. Humbly asked Him to remove our shortcomings. 8. Made a list of all persons we had harmed, and became willing to make amends to them all. 9. Made direct amends to such people wherever possible, except when to do so would Injure them or others. 10. Continued to take personal inventory and when we were wrong promptly admitted it. 11. Sought through prayer and meditation to Improve our conscious contact with God, as we understood Him, praying only for knowledge of His will for us and the power to carry that out. 12. Having had a spiritual awakening as the result of these steps, we tried to carry this message to alcoholics, and to practice these principles In all our affairs.

The Twelve Steps are reprinted with permission of Alcoholics Anonymous World Service, Inc. Permission to reprint and adapt the Twelve Steps does not mean that A.A.Is In any way affiliated with this program.A.A.Is a program of recovery from alcoholism - use of the Twelve Steps in connection with programs and activities which are patterned after A.A., but which address other problems, does not imply otherwise.

Step One:

"We admitted we were powerless over the enemy. fear. and that our lives had become unmanageable."

Our Higher Power, the Lord Jesus Christ, tells us in John 15:5, "I am the vine, ye are the branches: He that abideth in me, and I in him, the same bringeth forth much fruit: for without me ye can do nothing."

For many of us suffering from phobias and panic attacks, it took many years to finally admit our complete powerlessness. Our fear seemed too humiliating; we were embarrassed to admit this was something we could not control. Our lives became unmanageable, as we tried many ways, on our own, to control our fears.

When we admitted complete defeat, we were ready to receive the supernatural help of our Higher Power, Jesus Christ. When we came to Jesus with our fears and shortcomings, in humility and repentance, learning of Him, we felt we were no longer alone. We no longer had to fight this disorder on our own.

Indeed, on our own we were powerless over our fears, but now we have a power greater than ourselves. As we align our lives with His will for us, we find that we are in tune with divine order and harmony, perfect love, justice, perfect peace, goodness, and an outworking of all circumstances.

We are instructed to cast all of our cares upon Him, for He cares for us. Jesus is the Great Physician, the Burden Bearer. He has already defeated sin, disease, and death. He tells us we should be of good cheer for He has overcome the world.

We look to Jesus for guidance. He delivers us from the darkness of fear and despair, and through His Holy Spirit guides us into the light. He is the Way, the Truth, and the Life.

Jesus stands at the door and knocks. We need to make the choice to open the door and let Him in. He is our Redeemer and has completed our salvation on the cross. It is up to us to accept His gift of eternal life. When we do, we are born again spiritually, into a new life in Christ. The old with all of its fears and defects is gone. We are willing to leave behind the old thinking habits and become willing to be transformed by the renewing of our minds. We let the truth of God's love replace our old false beliefs and delusions. We make a choice not to live according to the flesh, but by the Spirit of God.

Because we are now joint heirs with Christ, we know

who we are. We are children of God, dearly loved. "For God so loved the world that He sent His only begotten Son, so whosoever believeth in Him should not perish, but have eternal life."

We are no longer powerless, for Jesus, our Higher Power, strengthens us. He has promised never to leave us nor forsake us. As we conform each day to His likeness, our lives are changed. We are saved, redeemed, transformed and renewed. We begin to walk by faith, not by fear.

Taking this First Step is the beginning of a new life. It is a relief in and of itself to give up the pretenses, the defenses and the self-deceptions. We are no longer alone.

We thank You, Lord Jesus, for meeting us at our point of need. You love and accept us just as we are. We don't need to earn your approval. Thank You for lifting our burden of phobias and panic attacks, as we put them into Your hands. We choose to rest in Your healing, all-powerful love.

Through the name of Jesus Christ, we are more than conquerors. Our delusions or false beliefs stemming from self condeming lies and irrational fears, are defeated foes. Jesus is the Truth and the Truth sets us free.

Step Two:

"We came to believe that a power greater than ourselves. the Lord Jesus Christ could restore us to sanity."

Recovering phobics have been so negatively programmed in their thinking, that recovery involves a complete transformation of the thinking process. What we think reflects what we believe; subsequently our lives reflect our thinking. Negative, fearful thinking causes us to have a distorted perspective of reality. Justice, truth, beauty and love become clouded in delusory beliefs. Fear caused us to buy into a lie, a deception, a false belief. When we look to our Higher Power, Jesus Christ, we see the truth. By the power of His Holy Spirit, we are led into the light.

This Second Step requires first a willingness to believe, a belief in God. Many of us begin in total unbelief; many of us have distorted beliefs; and all of us can increase the strength of our belief. We then need to comprehend that our Higher Power, Jesus, can restore us. When we study the life, the teachings and the gospel of Jesus Christ, His power to restore us is made evident. As we choose to follow Him, He restores us. We choose this, by faith, one day at a time.

All power in Heaven and Earth is given to Jesus. He is the beginning and the end, the Alpha and the Omega. He healed the sick, restored sight to the blind, raised the dead, cast out demons, subdued nature and victoriously rose from the dead. Yes, Jesus has the power to restore us suffering phobics to sanity, wholeness and health. As we conform more and more to His likeness, through the sanctification process, we become holy. Holiness, wholeness, and healthiness all reflect the victory that is in Christ.

When we truly believe that Jesus can restore our health and wholeness, we will allow Him to. We will drop the reins of self-will and self-control. We will relinquish our attempts to manipulate a cure, an escape, or a cover-up for our affliction. We will let God take control and rest in His healing power.

Oftentimes the endless commitments and responsibilities of everyday life make it difficult to slow down, to be still and to know God. We cannot exercise a proper communication with our Higher Power, without taking time to commune with Him. Jesus Christ should be our number one priority, for He is our greatest need on this Earth. It is important to spend time with Him, reading the scriptures, praying and thinking about what He has done for us. We must keep our eyes to the Heavens for Jesus says, "Follow me".

Step Three:

"We made a decision to turn our will and our lives over to the care of God the Father, His Son Jesus Christ and His Holy Spirit."

When we recovering phobics take time to reflect on nature, on life, and the universe, we become aware that there is a continuity to everything. The days, the seasons, the wave cycle, the rotation of the planets around the sun all portray the order and consistency which God intended. We, too, can lead ordered, harmonious lives. But first, we need to let go of our own self-will. We need to be in harmony with God and His great love, power and energy.

In Step Three, we surrender. We relinquish control of our lives. We ask the Lord Jesus Christ to be our Savior and Guide. We turn over our anxieties and fears to Him. We rest in Him knowing that He is all-powerful and loving. We learn to trust in Him. No longer do we demand things on our time schedule. We establish faith by trusting in God's timing, in His all-powerful omnipresence. He sees the end from the beginning and desires for us only what is right, good and just. We are His children. If we trust in Him and His everlasting love for us, we can rest assured that all will be well. Many of our fears and anxieties would be alleviated if we just gave up control and put God in charge of our lives. When we fret and become frustrated, we should remember to relax - God is in charge.

Through our surrender to our Higher Power, Jesus Christ, we will also become more patient. Our impulsive and compulsive behaviors diminish as we realize that we are not only complicating our lives, but we are also causing undue stress and poor results.

We learn to give praise and thanks to God for His redemption work and for His transforming power in us. We are aware of the freedom we are gaining through the sanctification process of salvation. We accept the Holy Spirit dwelling in us as our guide, counselor, and purifier. Thank You, Lord Jesus, for saving us. Thank You for delivering us. We give you praise and honor, and seek to glorify Your name. We are no longer alone in our struggle against fear and panic, but have been adopted into our Heavenly Father's family. We are children of God, dearly loved. Jesus promised before His Crucifixion, "I will not leave you comfortless. I will come to you."

By taking Step Three, we make ourselves open and

receptive to the Comforter, His Holy Spirit. Little by little, the dreaded fear responses are replaced with God's peace. Our serenity increases as we yield our will and let God take control-as we cast our cares upon Him.

The key to the turning point involved in this step is that it requires a decision. As children of God, made in His image, we have creative abilities. This requires freedom. We are free to make a choice. No one can force us to do this. If we choose to accept Jesus as our Savior, and surrender our lives to Him, we allow His transforming love and power to enter our lives. At that point, we are born again as new creations in Christ. All our old self-defeating habits and fears begin to die and we begin to walk in resurrection life. Walking out of our old habit patterns and walking in the newness of resurrection life is a process that we journey through one day at a time. Yes, we may relapse at times into negative, fearful thinking, but we must stop these thoughts as soon as we can. We must avoid doubt, confusion, fear and despair and focus on things that are lovely, good, right, beautiful and truthful. We must focus on Jesus. Our minds become renewed as we receive more and more of God's grace.

Step Four:

"We made a searching and fearless moral inventory of ourselves."

We recovering phobics had made such a habit of focusing on our fears, our circumstances, and other people's problems, that we rarely spent time on self-knowledge. Our insight had been clouded by doubt and fear. We were in the darkness. We were deceived by the world and became self deceived. We found in surrendering our lives to Jesus Christ, that we were walking out of darkness into the light. The Holy Spirit was shining light on us so that our perception became real. Our delusions and dependencies no longer worked to allow us to avoid the Truth.

As we begin to walk in the light, it can be a very painful experience to see our faults more clearly. But we must remember that this is God's way of refining us, of making us pure and holy. We thought we could handle our fears, panic attacks, and dependencies ourselves, but we found out that we were powerless. Without our Higher Power, our Lord and Savior Jesus Christ, we could do nothing.

This Fourth Step allows us to take an honest look at

ourselves, both our good points and our faults. Instead of spending our time avoiding reality through various compulsive behaviors, or by blaming circumstances or other people; we look in the mirror. We focus on ourselves, in relationship to our Heavenly Father and His will for us. We are His children and we begin to see the areas where we are not in alignment with His all-powerful love and goodness. We begin to get right with God.

To take a personal and fearless moral inventory we need to take the time to find a quiet, serene place where we will be able to really focus and get an accurate perception of ourselves. This requires getting away from the hustle and bustle of everyday life, separating from the demands made on us by other people or work obligations. It requires cutting off all of the artificial stimuli we are bombarded with each day - televisions, telephones, fax machines, computers, etc. It means we must detach from unhealthy dependencies that cloud our thinking. Such dependencies include chemicals such as alcohol and drugs; but they also include abnormal dependencies on other people, work, money and so on.

When we have achieved the solitude, serenity, and soberness of mind, we are ready to take an accurate inventory.

Because we are constantly growing and changing through the power of the Holy Spirit and the sanctification process, we will need to take a personal inventory often. It is like peeling the layers off an onion. We continually see more and more, the deeply buried aspects of ourselves coming to the surface. All of the old negative, fearful, often sinful thinking and behavior habits become apparent, allowing our Higher Power to work in us to remove them.

It often takes many years to arrive at the point of being willing to take an honest personal inventory. It is only after we have repeated the same mistakes over and over again that we realize we had better stop and take a closer look at our lives. We can no longer keep blaming the past, other people, lack of money or other things. We need to free ourselves to move onward and upward in our spiritual growth. As we do this we find ourselves being set free. We no longer want to be sick and tired. We are sick and tired of being sick and tired. We are ready for change and we must always remember that our Higher Power, Jesus Christ and His Holy Spirit are right here within us to help. Our Higher Power saves us, heals us, delivers us and transforms our lives. For this we give Him praise and are eternally grateful.

Beginning a moral inventory involves putting our perceptions in writing. In this way we are able to be more objective and better able to deal with what we see. We want to be sure that we consider our assets as well as our liabilities. We should be very loving and forgiving to ourselves and realize that we did the best we were capable of at the time. Jesus forgives us, and we should forgive ourselves.

Jesus bore our guilt and shame on the cross when He died for us. The guilt and shame of our sins were buried with Him. Through Christ's resurrection, we are born again—new creations, living a new life.

As phobics, we recognize that fear was one of our defects of character, a major soul-sickness. Its vice-like grip on our lives, blocked out or made difficult the life affirming assets of belief, faith, hope, trust, and love.

Having admitted our irrational fears and our powerlessness over them, gave us a starting point from which to examine our lives honestly and take our much needed inventory. We can compare this to cleaning out a cluttered room.

In taking inventory, we may have realized that unbelief was also one of our defects. We found it difficult perhaps to believe in God who is all good, but even more so, to believe that He loves us. We did not believe in ourselves. We were burdened with low self-worth and self-esteem. We not only had a distorted view of God's character, but also of ourselves. Many of us did not have an accurate self perception at all. Motivated by fear and insecurity, our vision was obscured. Our good points were clouded over by our false perceptions and false beliefs.

Many suffering phobics became depressed and found that this defect of character stopped constructive action. Depression lead to anti-life thoughts and choices. Sadly, some situations ended in suicide. We cannot discount or minimize the deadly consequences of our disorder. We must seek help. God is good and when we walk with Him, He brings order out of disorder-He places our feet on a Rock. We, who are blessed so much, need to bring hope and help to other suffering phobics. Through absolute faith and trust in our Higher Power, we know that divine order and harmony do exist and that God, in His time, will bring good to us. He loves us! We cannot see through the veils to the souls who have departed while still in bondage to their fears, but we can rest assured that they are in another room now, learning about the freedom, the love and power and glory of our Lord.

Fear, unbelief, doubt, depression were all defects of character that needed to be uprooted. Upon examining ourselves, we may have found that we developed a variety of unhealthy dependencies or behavior patterns in trying to cope with our fears. The anesthetizing effects of alcohol or drugs often allowed us to feel less afraid, less inhibited. We often sought after other people to lean on. Many of us became co-dependent. We put too much emphasis on financial security and some of us became in bondage to money. What we found was that any substance or activity used in excess to placate our fears and insecurities often became another problem in itself. The substance or activity had become a form of idolatry. Perhaps alcohol abuse, sexual addiction, eating disorders, hoarding money, compulsively working or enabling behaviors developed. It was often only when any or all of these behaviors did not work to alleviate our fears and doubts, that we admitted defeat. It is at this point that we were ready to meet our Higher Power, Jesus Christ midway. When we come to Him and surrender our will and life to Him, we no longer have to fight these defects alone. He gives us the power to overcome our insecurities and flaws. We find that, one day at a time, He is transforming our lives. We need to have faith and trust in Him. God desires that we put Him first in our lives.

The emptiness or loneliness that some refer to as the "hole in the soul" cannot be filled with anything but the love of God. Let us come to Him, in our need, be still and wait patiently for Him. He is faithful and will heal us. We thank you, Lord Jesus. You are the Great Physician.

We discovered that we possessed many good qualities. We may have been victimized or traumatized by some life event which made us bitter. The sins of our fathers may have been passed down to us as we became recipients of ungodly or unholy behaviors. We may have compromised our own integrity. We may have turned to dishonest ways of accumulating wealth and financial security, having been very industrious and hard workers to begin with. We may have tried too hard to be loved, without reciprocation, causing us to resort to manipulative schemes. We were like a beautiful piece of china that had become chipped and cracked. Our Higher Power could restore that original work of art if we would let Him.

Having taken an honest moral inventory, we then are able to lay our defects at the foot of the cross. They are buried with our old self. Through the blood of Jesus, we are cleansed from all sin. We are forgiven. Through His resurrection and our baptism, we are given a new life in Christ. We praise God and give Him thanks.

Step Five:

"We admitted to God, to ourselves and to another human being the exact nature of our wrongs."

As we journey through the Twelve Steps, we move from darkness into the light. As more light is shown, we become aware of and see our defects. We gain insight. Having seen our wrongs more clearly, we need to confess them. We cannot carry around secrets for we found that people are as sick as their secrets. We unburden ourselves · when we admit our wrongs.

In admitting our wrongs to God, we ask Him to forgive us and He does. God waits patiently for us to come to Him and repent. He desires that we live a new righteous life. Our God seeks the lost and is very concerned to bring us back home to Him. He understands our weaknesses and stands ready to welcome us back into the fold. We found that our wrongs had truly separated us from the presence of God. We had been lost. But when we come to Christ, admit our wrongs, ask forgiveness, and truly desire to change, He gives us grace.

We phobics often felt a lot of guilt and shame over

our fears and unhealthy behaviors. We need to remember that God loves us. When we bring our wrongs to Him, He forgives us and He forgets. We should also forgive ourselves and not dwell on past sins. Christ paid the price to redeem us. He died on the cross for our sins, and we do not need to continually berate nor condemn ourselves anymore. We no longer need to feel guilt and shame for we are new creations in Christ. Our old selves have died and our new selves live unto Christ. His Holy Spirit dwells in us. We do not act in our own power or adequacy anymore. We act through faith in the power of God within us.

We can be victims of self-deception when it comes to fully confessing our wrongs. We sometimes are in denial as to our true motives. We need to pray for God's Holy Spirit to guide us and lead us into Truth. We need to be willing to admit our wrongs, even if we don't fully see them yet. It takes time to clean out a house. The emotional clutter and excess baggage we've carried around is not usually removed in a moment. As we throw out the more obvious clutter, we may find hidden defects underneath.

Talking to a trusted friend is very helpful. It is in relating our wrongs to another human being, that our own perceptions become clearer and accurate. In talking, we actually work out some of the issues that are hurting us. We need to select an individual with spiritual maturity who will not use our disclosures to harm us. We can pray that God will bring us a trusted confidant.

This Fifth Step says we admit the exact nature of our wrongs. The word exact suggests that we do not try to sugar-coat nor cover over some of our wrongs. We need to courageously look at the exact nature of our wrongs. We will feel shame and guilt, but these are part of repenting. After repenting, we leave shame and guilt behind.

We need to remember that we are imperfect human beings in an imperfect world. We cannot be perfect on our own. God is compassionate, merciful, and forgiving to us as we need to be to ourselves and to others.

Step Six:

"We became entirely ready to have God remove our defects of character."

What does becoming "ready" mean? We look at Step Six and desire to become ready for God to remove our shortcomings. By working the steps, we already show that we do have a desire to improve. We had found that none of our old ways released us from the bondage of fear, phobias, and panic attacks. We were usually in bondage to other dependencies too, perhaps alcohol or drugs, codependency, or possessions. We were tired of our self-defeating behavior patterns.

Becoming ready involves admitting our own personal powerlessness. It means breaking out of denial and seeing that our lives have become unmanageable. Once we realize that we, by ourselves, are incapable of solving our own problems, then we are ready to ask for help. For our God to remove our shortcomings, we need to believe. Many of us held false beliefs or unbelief. To be ready requires us to learn of our Higher Power, Jesus Christ. As we learn of Him, we come to believe in His power to deliver us.

Because we have been beaten down by irrational fears,

it was easy to relapse into negative fearful thinking. Our thought patterns had been full of doubt, mistrust and despair. We had to replace these negative thought patterns with positive thoughts of good, faith, love, hope and truth. As we focus on Jesus Christ, we change our thinking patterns, based on our Higher Power's love for us. He has overcome the tribulations of this world, and in Him, we too are overcomers. By belief in Him and faith in His love and power in our lives, we are victorious over phobias and unhealthy dependencies.

Acquiring and strengthening our belief takes time. We need to practice our belief, faith, trust, and hope on a daily basis, or we will regress to the old fearful thought processes. Scripture says, "Be transformed by the renewal of your minds." One day at a time, our thinking is transformed.

To be ready for God to do His work in our lives to deliver us, we need to let Him be in charge. Because of our immense level of fear and insecurity, we, phobics, had liked to control the people or situations in our lives. We felt safe when we were in control. But that did not work. It was unfair to expect someone else to fulfill all our own desires. We found we needed to become personally responsible for our own recovery, happiness and quality of life. The only person we could utterly depend on was God. Depending on other people or things to make us happy became a form of idolatry. Our God wants our love and allegiance to Him first and foremost. He is our Creator, and we are His children. Jesus is our Shepherd and we are His sheep. We are to look to Him for guidance. He has promised never to leave us nor forsake us. He came to give us abundant life.

Being ready for God to work in eradicating our defects means that we need to give up our obstinate self will. Because of our fears, we phobics had been afraid that our needs and wants would not be met. We lacked faith in God and in ourselves. We either tried too hard to have our own way or didn't try at all. We found that our will did not bear positive results. We had to surrender our will to our Higher Power's will for us. He knows what is best for us. He loves us and desires to give us whatever we ask if it is good and right for us. He sees the end from the beginning and will work out all things for the best.

To yield our own will is a frightening thing. It left us in doubt, feeling out of control and helpless. Some asked what if there is no God? What if He doesn't answer my prayers?

What if I've done too many bad things? What if I have to give up everything? We go on and on catastrophizing. It takes time to break this obsession of negative thinking. As we continually surrender our will to His will, He gives us grace. Little by little, a day at a time, we see that God is doing for us what we could not do for ourselves.

From sheer habit and lingering fear, we will still take up the reins of control and try to direct our lives. We will probably try to direct other's lives too, become domineering. We then need to step back and "Let go and let God." To deal with our insecurities we had adopted compulsive behaviors. Some of us felt that if we just did more, worked more, exercised more, gave more, etc., etc., then we'd be okay. Our compulsive behavior just wore us out. God's gift of freedom and serenity is free. We do not need to earn it.

Paradoxically, being ready for God to remove our shortcomings doesn't mean we need to do more, be more, feel guilty, try harder to engineer the solutions or to figure things out. Being ready means to become humble, to submit to our Lord, to believe in Him, to trust in Him, to have faith in His power to heal and to be still before Him. To receive our deliverance, let us come before the Lord, give him our burdens and wait patiently for Him to heal us. God is faithful to keep His promises. Let us receive His all powerful healing love.

Step Seven:

"*We humbly asked Him to remove our shortcomings.*"

When we suffering phobics came to an end of ourselves and to our attempts at self-care, we were in a position to ask God to work. We had to be ready and willing to let God heal. Our Higher Power, Jesus Christ, has all power and authority over disease. In His name, there is healing of our diseases and deliverance from evil. Our part is to believe, to have faith, to trust and to obey.

In taking this step, we put aside our doubts, fears and attempts to control. We humbly ask Him to remove our shortcomings. We give Him praise and thanks and rest patiently. We remain still and quiet before the Lord. We accept and receive His love, grace, and healing. We remain steadfast and firm in our faith. We stand on the rock of Jesus Christ. When old habit thought patterns attack our minds, we focus on Jesus. We abstain from sinful thoughts and behaviors. We recognize doubt and confusion as enemies, and we avoid them.

We need to take this step simply. Having a pure heart and right motives, we ask God to help us with our shortcomings.

Being freed of these defects, we are more able to share our Higher Power, Jesus, His gospel, His love, and His redemptive and transforming power and His victory.

We may be tempted to try too hard in this step. Let us remember that God knows our hearts, our defects, our desires and needs. He loves us and wants to give us full life. He has promised us that if we ask, we will receive.

We thank You, Lord Jesus, for healing us. We humbly ask that you remove our defects of character that stand in the way of our usefulness to you and our fellow human beings. We wait patiently for you and let go of the reins. We trust in You, Lord, and walk by faith.

Each day, one day at a time, let's keep it simple. Let us give our burdens to Jesus. Let us trust in Him. Let us obey His commandments and rest in the Lord. After we have taken this step, let us daily "let go and let God". Thank You, Lord. Let us remember that the victory in Phobics Victorious is in Jesus. Our personal victory comes through faith and trust in Christ.

Step Eight:

"We made a list of all persons we had harmed and became willing to make amends to them all."

When we recovering phobics review our life choices, behaviors, and patterns, we find that we were motivated primarily by our fear and insecurity. Because of our fear, we often hurt other people. We may have either hung on too closely, trying to control and manipulate them, or we did not ever enter into loving intimate relationships at all. Often when in relationships, we acted unwisely because of fear. Perhaps our tremendous fear of abandonment and rejection kept us in unhealthy relationships that were self-destructive. Or perhaps we could not get past the fear into really loving and trusting another.

Many of us had placed our love and trust in the wrong place. We looked to money to fill our needs. Or we looked to alcohol, drugs, or sex to dull the fear and pain. Unhealthy addictive behaviors developed that hurt not only ourselves, but also others. We found that fear became a bondage which kept us from being free to love unconditionally.

Having a greater understanding of our past behaviors

and being willing to admit our mistakes and take personal responsibility leads us to making amends. We could not make amends before when we were too busy blaming everyone else or our circumstances, or when we were too paralyzed by fear to take any action.

Now we have come to a place in our spiritual growth where we are able to look honestly at our past actions. We are becoming more bold in reconciling broken, hurt relationships. Through God's grace we are being reconciled to Him and to ourselves, and we are being healed. We are becoming ministers of reconciliation.

Let us make a list of people we have hurt. It is important not to be too hard on ourselves. It takes two in relationships and often we may have taken on undue responsibility for any problems. Because of our fear, we may have tried too hard. We may have been people pleasers. We may have felt a lot of false guilt and shame at our unmanageable life. So let's try to look objectively at ourselves and where we truly did hurt someone else, we can become willing to make amends.

We should also realize that we have hurt ourselves. In order to heal, we need to make amends to ourselves. We need to realize we did the best we could for what we knew.

We should forgive ourselves as God forgives us. We need to love ourselves and treat ourselves well and with respect. We need to be gentle and patient with ourselves. We can make healthy choices for ourselves, and experience love, goodness and beauty. We need to accept God's free gift of life and learn to celebrate and enjoy it. Making amends to ourselves involves feeling God's love for us and learning to love ourselves. It includes learning to take gentle good care of ourselves. Fear, guilt, anger, resentment, doubt, despair only pull us down and block the beauty within each of us. So let us be sure to put ourselves high on our list of people we have harmed. We no longer want to self-destruct. We want to live and love and enjoy. We learn to tenderly make choices that are loving, healthy and good for us. We learn we are valuable, worthwhile, highly esteemed Children of God.

Becoming willing to make amends to others we have hurt takes courage. Because of our fear, we are afraid to go to people we have hurt. They may reject us or get angry with us. They may not even care or want any communication with us. But part of our making amends is for our welfare too. We ask for forgiveness. We forgive. We let go of past mistakes. We cannot afford to have stored up resentment, anger, bitterness or guilt. All these emotions are destructive and lead to disease. To be truly happy and healthy and free, we need to rid ourselves of any negative thoughts and emotions. We don't want to carry around excess baggage from the past. We are doing our part, with the help of the Holy Spirit, to purify ourselves and thereby truly enjoy the gift of life. We know that as God through Christ forgives us, we should forgive others.

Step Nine:

"We made direct amends to such people whenever possible. except when to do so would injure them or others."

Step nine is an action step. It requires that we do something. Because of our phobic responses, we have often acquired avoidant behavior patterns. The fear and the fear of our fear was so predominant in our minds that we chose not to act. We often became paralyzed, unable to function normally. Panic attacks have a way of paralyzing a person's ability to function spontaneously. We do not unlearn these avoidant behavior patterns overnight. Through the grace of God, we are able to take little baby steps, one day at a time, in acting boldly, fearlessly, and courageously.

We admitted our problems and made a decision to change. Repentance means to change one's mind. We wanted God to remove our defects of character, predominantly unhealthy fear, and we wanted to do His will. We found that repenting involved changing the way we think, believe, live. We could not accomplish this transformation without the help of the Holy Spirit. But we did have to "do" something. This is where making amends to our Higher Power and to ourselves comes first.

God loves us. We are His children. He has taught us through the scriptures and through His Son, Jesus Christ, what we need to do to live joyously and abundantly in fellowship with Him and each other. Yet through sin, we have separated ourselves from the holiness of God. Sin blinded us. Our own disobedience, self-will, rebelliousness and sinful choices brought about our negative consequences. Therefore, we need to make amends to our Higher Power by bringing ourselves and our sins to the cross. Through the blood of Christ we are cleansed from all sin. We die with Christ to our old sinful self and we rise with Christ to a resurrection life. Now it is up to us to choose to follow Jesus one day at time. Through His power and strength, we overcome the negative, sinful, habit patterns.

We must learn to love ourselves the way our Heavenly Father loves us. We have been bruised and battered from sin, and we need healing. We can make amends to ourselves by being very gentle, loving, and kind to ourselves. We can choose to only follow Jesus, to do what is right and good, to not choose any action that is outside the will of God. We can choose not to harm our bodies or our minds in any way. We make choices that honor our personal dignity and that show self-respect. We can become healthy, holy and sanctified little by little, a day at a time. Thank you, Lord, for giving us your Holy Spirit, to guide us and lead us into all truth.

We need to keep in mind that we are only able to love and make amends to others as we love and make amends to God and to ourselves. Then we are able to act out of healthy loving motives, not out of fear and selfishness. When we truly believe that God loves us that we are forgiven through Christ, and that we have the Holy Spirit in us, then we can love ourselves. We will want to act only in ways that are good and best for us. We do not want to hang on to unforgiveness, anger, resentment, bitterness, unholy behaviors. This is where making amends to others helps rid ourselves of any negative self-destructive emotions. We cannot always guarantee that our amends will be accepted with love and reconciliation. But we will know we did our part.

Let us in prayer and meditation, seek God's will in making amends to others. Let Him guide us. We don't want to plow into sensitive situations and engineer solutions that could open old wounds or cause more harm. We want to use gentleness, quietness and sensitivity in reaching out to others in making amends. We want to be able to see through their character defects to the child of God that they are. We want to be compassionate and understanding that all of us have acted in unloving ways through our own being hurt, our own anger and fear.

Often a note expressing our apology is sufficient. Sometimes a get-together to share verbally is appropriate. We often need to give back something if theft is involved. Whatever way we choose to make amends the most important part is that we act in love and humility and unconditionally. God forgave us through His Son Jesus Christ so we should forgive others likewise.

We need to realize that the Holy Spirit will shed more and more light on us, and we will see more areas that were unclean and sinful. We need to deal with these areas, confessing, forsaking, reconciling, so we can move on. We are in the process of cleaning our house, of sanctification. Let us not become too despondent as we see these negative areas, for it is in seeing and feeling the pain that we are led to freedom.

Step Ten:

"Continued to take a daily personal inventory and when we were wrong, promptly admitted it."

In Phobics Victorious we are learning, one day at a time, to live a new way of life. We no longer want irrational fears and subsequent behaviors to ruin our lives. We work the twelve steps as a format or program. We are letting go of unhealthy dependencies and learning to depend on God. We are giving up self-will and trusting in the will of God. We are leading honest lives, and facing reality truthfully. We are no longer letting delusions and self-deceptions destroy our lives.

Each day we take a few moments to honestly reflect on our thoughts and actions. Where we have been wrong, we quickly admit it. We are in the process of becoming pure and holy. We do not desire to have any garbage in our lives.

It is important for us recovering phobics not to be too hard on ourselves in recovery. Once we see the light and realize our self-defeating thoughts and behaviors, we become very anxious to get well. We need to realize that we did not get sick overnight and we will not get well overnight.

We need to be very patient with ourselves and when we do slip and relapse, we need to forgive ourselves and keep going on. We know that each morning is a new day and a new beginning. Our hope is in the Lord Jesus Christ and His power within us to transform. Let's keep it simple and trust in Him each day. If we put one foot in front of the other and choose only what is right, we will grow into spiritual health and maturity. God is faithful to keep His promises and to be with us all the way.

Taking a daily inventory keeps us honest. It is easy to let our little self-deceptions and our denial of reality to block the truth. We cannot afford to do wrong or keep secrets. As we clean up our lives, our fears slip away. We are able to honestly look others in the eye. We have nothing to hide. Because we live surrendered lives and have our Higher Power in us, we do not have to hide or be afraid. We are part of life and its eternal ebb and flow.

Upon retiring at night it is a good idea to do a quick self-evaluation. We are not perfect and will make mistakes. In fact, because we are now walking in the light not in the darkness, we will see our defects more clearly, and it will hurt. We will feel shame and remorse, but we know we are forgiven through our Higher Power, Jesus Christ.

So let's not be too hard on ourselves. Growing up spiritually and emotionally is a process. God loves us and desires our fellowship with Him. Obedience and submission to Him is for our best interest. Let us look to Him as a loving Heavenly Father who desires only good, loving and abundant life for His children. Let us not let guilt, shame, and self-condemnation keep us from this abundant life. We are new creations in Christ, and He desires to give us joy.

Step Eleven:

"We sought through prayer and meditation to improve our conscious contact with God the Father, His Son Jesus Christ, and His Holy Spirit, praying only for knowledge of His will for us and the power to carry that out."

Because phobias and panic attacks left us so powerless, we often adopted negative or inadequate ways to cope. We tried to control our circumstances so we would not be so afraid. We often acquired compulsive behaviors to numb the fear and pain. We often became too busy to feel our feelings. We used various methods to avoid and run from our fear. Some of us used alcohol or drugs, or compulsive work habits, or co-dependent relationships, or spending or acquiring and so on. But when these methods did not offer relief, we admitted defeat and turned to our Higher Power for help.

Step eleven is the step that offers us access to our Higher Power's help. This step requires that we seek our Higher Power through prayer and meditation. In Phobics Victorious, we adopt this as a way of life. When we find that we are going astray or losing our focus and our serenity, we have probably been neglecting step eleven.

It is very easy in today's society to not take time for prayer and meditation. We have many responsibilities, and life seems to move so fast. Yet if we're not careful to practice step eleven, we can easily become disoriented, confused, and worn out.

Our Higher Power, the Lord Jesus Christ often pulled away from the crowd for quiet communion with His Father. He did not feel guilty about leaving the everyday world. He knew it was a necessity. He also fasted during some of His times with His Father. He was not only cleansing His body, but was also nourishing His spirit. We can often get so caught up with meeting our physical needs that they take priority over the spiritual. God wants to feed our spirit.

It is a beneficial practice to begin the day in prayer. An attitude of gratitude sets an optimistic tone. Upon awakening, we thank our Higher Power for this day and all of our blessings. Counting our blessing helps us to focus on what we do have. We surrender our life and this day to the Lord and pray to do His will. The Holy Spirit is so near to give us the strength and the power and to guide us. We need to always remember that there is power in the name of Jesus and that we can come to Him in prayer and use His Holy name. Our belief and faith will grow and grow and our fear will dissipate.

We often live through the day with a quiet heart of prayer. We adopt a stance of petitioning the Lord - of looking to Him.

Meditation helps us to learn and focus on God's will. God speaks to us through His Holy Scriptures. We will find the right answers and guidance we need when we spend time meditating on the scriptures. Lessons can also be learned by meditating on aspects of nature. Nature reveals so clearly the cycle of life, the order and harmony. Nature reveals power and energy in things we cannot see with our eyes.

There is power in prayer, more than we are able to understand. It is appropriate to pray for others. Phobics Victorious is a fellowship, and we offer our prayers for all those suffering and in recovery. Our Higher Power tells us that where two or three are gathered together in His name, He is in the midst of us. How very powerful. Our Higher Power heals!

In our prayer and meditation, we don't need to work at it or try too hard. We need to adopt a trusting, believing attitude and take it very easy. We are yielding to our God.

He knows our heart and mind. We can align ourselves with Him, give Him the reins of control, and go with the flow. Let us always have faith in the process of life and in the triumph of love over fear.

We pray that the Holy Spirit will show us how to pray and will lead us into the very presence of God. We also pray that we will use the name of Jesus in the healing and deliverance of our fears according to the will of God. Higher Power show us the way!

Step Twelve:

"Having had a spiritual awakening as a result of these steps. we tried to carry this message to others and to practice its principles in all of our affairs."

Our program for recovery is for sharing. Phobics Victorious is a fellowship. In this fellowship we are all equal. We help each other by sharing our experience, strength, and hope. We are also given the privilege to share about the good news of Jesus Christ. In sharing about our Higher Power, Jesus Christ, we are ministers of the gospel. We are involved in the work of evangelism. Phobics Victorious is a means to take the gospel into the world.

We have found in our own lives that the twelve steps, with Jesus as our Higher Power, brings healing. This is a spiritual program and through following Jesus and practicing the principles in the twelve steps, we are delivered from our fears. The love of Christ through the power of His Holy Spirit has replaced our fears. This spiritual experience referred to in step twelve, happens in a variety of ways and durations of time, yet in all instances we are given a gift, an awareness of our oneness with God, of His love for us, and of His very closeness to us. We are made aware of the victory of life over death, peace over confusion, health over disease. We are hooked into the peace of God, the power of His might, the order and harmony of His creation. We are made to realize that we can do all things through Christ who strengthens us.

We begin to live a life based on belief and faith not one based on fear. We try, one day at a time, to make choices that are in alignment with God, life and love, with what is righteous and good.

Little by little we find that our lives are becoming more ordered, more honest and pure. We find that we are not trying to control everyone and everything. We are trusting in God. Our relationship with our Higher Power becomes the most important and then our relationship with ourselves. We are then able to come together in fellowship with other phobics and nourish each other. We don't desire to control them, run the show, or selfishly seek our own will. We let the love of God flow through us.

Support group meetings offer a convenient way to fellowship and share with each other. We can also share the message and practice the twelve steps wherever we are –

at home, work, church, abroad. We are never alone for our Higher Power has said "Lo, I am with you always."

It is necessary to remember to work our own program, not someone else's. We cannot force someone else's spiritual experience to happen when we want it to. We need to keep our focus on Jesus and our own recovery. It is natural to want to help others recover and we can share our experience, strength and hope. But we cannot control another nor manipulate their recovery. Each one of us grows in a different way and at a different rate. God is in charge, not us. When we're disappointed that our loved ones and friends aren't catching the program fast enough for us, we need to "Let go and let God" and to "Live and let live." This can be frightening for phobics because we've been so insecure. But now we are learning to trust in God. Our responsibility is our own recovery. By working the twelve steps, accepting Jesus as our Savior, we are led into a position to glorify God. We become cleaner, more pure, truthful, and channels of God's love and life.

The twelve steps are a life long program for living. They keep us on track. Let us incorporate their principles into our lives one day at a time. All the aspects of reality, of our being are inclusive in just one day. Let us look to each day in obedience, be faithful to the present moment, be mindful to the task at hand, do the next right thing in front of us and trust in God. He is with us at all times. He loves us. He is faithful and just. He will keep His promises. He is merciful and compassionate and kind. He forgives us and gives us new life and resurrection power. We give you thanks and praise, Lord Jesus, and desire to glorify you in our lives.

Through the power of Jesus Christ we can live life as victors, not victims. If you do not know Jesus as your Lord and Savior, you can ask Him into your life today. He is the Burden Bearer, the Great Physician. He says to "Come unto Me", "Ask and it shall be given," "Seek and you shall find."

Jesus invites you to come to Him. To accept this invitation pray, "Lord Jesus, I come to you. I bring you my defects of character. I leave them at the cross. I accept you as my Lord and Savior. I surrender my will and my life to you. Come into my heart and guide me through your Holy Spirit. I give you thanks and praise. In the name of Jesus, Amen."

How To Conduct A Phobics Victorious Meeting

In Phobics Victorious support group meetings we concentrate on the Twelve Steps of Phobics Victorious, on the Holy Scriptures, on our meditation text, *One Day at a Time in Phobics Victorious* and first and foremost, we focus on Jesus!

For suffering phobics wishing to fellowship with each other in Phobics Victorious support group meetings, the following information is helpful.

As there are no leaders, just trusted servants, the trusted servant initiating a Phobics Victorious meeting, should pick a location, a time of day, 1 to 2 hours, once a week and should place information in a local newspaper, on fliers, etc.

The group facilitator gains trust by acknowledging that all information shared at meetings is strictly confidential. People meet to share their experience, strength and hope.

The format is flexible. Either a step can be studied. A page or pages from the *One Day at a Time in Phobics Victorious* can be discussed.

One successful format is to open with a prayer. The facilitator introduces himself or herself and each participant shares his/her first name only. The twelve steps are read. The introduction in *One Day at a Time in Phobics Victorious* is read. The facilitator tells a little bit about him or herself - phobias, panic attacks, positive testimonies.

The group then discusses the topic; a step, a meditation, a subject out of the program such as powerlessness, belief, surrender, etc. Several Holy Scriptures can be discussed.

The last half of the meeting is open to free group sharing on a voluntary basis. At the close, prayer requests are made and the participants join together in prayer.

A basket is passed for a voluntary donation usually, a dollar, to help cover housing, refreshment costs.

Individual Phobics Victorious groups can prepare phonelists for the participants, so each can seek assistance between meetings.

Phobics Victorious is here to proclaim the name of Jesus as Lord and Savior and High Power. Phobics Victorious is here to offer love and hope and healing in the Spirit of our fellowship.

We invite you to come to Jesus, to learn of Him. We invite you to fellowship with other recovering phobics in Phobics Victorious meetings. Start a meeting. It only takes two. We pray that God's grace will rest on you and that His Holy Spirit will guide you into Truth and Freedom.

Please find more books by Rosemary on amazon.com:

Jesus, My Higher Power

The Twelve Steps of Phobics Anonymous

One Day at a Time in Phobics Victorious

www.ingramcontent.com/pod-product-compliance
Lightning Source LLC
Chambersburg PA
CBHW061515040426
42450CB00008B/1624